BILL COSBY

The Changing Black Image

by
Robert Rosenberg

New Directions
The Millbrook Press
Brookfield, Connecticut

Produced in Association with Agincourt Press.
Interior Design: Tilman Reitzle

Photographs courtesy of: AP/Wide World Photos: 6, 15, 25, 55, 56, 58, 61, 64, 84, 87; Michael Ochs Archives, Venice, CA: 33, 34, 38, 41, 42, 47, 66, 68, 73, 75, 77, 80; Milwaukee Sentinel: 36, 78; Schomburg Center for Research in Black Culture, N.Y. Public Library, Astor, Lenox and Tilden Foundations: 43.

Cataloging-in-Publication Data

Rosenberg, Robert.
Bill Cosby: the changing black image.

100 p.; ill.: (New directions)
Bibliography: p.
Includes index.

Summary: A biography of comedian Bill Cosby that explains how his personal form of humor helped move blacks into the mainstream of U.S. entertainment.

1. Cosby, Bill, 1937– 2. Television Actors and Actresses—Biography. I. Title. II. Series.

B (92)
ISBN 1-878841-17-3

Contents

Introduction

Bill Cosby—comedian, author, and movie star—is today one of the most trusted and admired figures in America. But there was a time not so long ago when this would have been impossible. As late as the 1960s, black people all over this country were denied jobs, political office, and even television stardom simply because of the color of their skin.

The civil rights movement of the 1950s and 1960s did much to change this situation so that a black man like Bill Cosby could succeed. Now, as Cliff Huxtable, the father and doctor he plays on "The Cosby Show," Cosby himself provides an important example to many black children, showing them that a black person can indeed achieve in American society. He has helped blacks to enter the mainstream of the entertainment industry, and his major financial contributions to Spelman College have done much to help a new generation of black women obtain a good education.

But Bill Cosby's success, like that of the family depicted on "The Cosby Show," is not a condition shared by many blacks in America. Most blacks have a harder time finding jobs and housing than whites, and blacks are much more likely to be poor. In fact, more than half of all black children in this country now live below the poverty line. And most blacks in America feel the impact of racism on a daily basis.

The fact that Bill Cosby and Cliff Huxtable have "made it" shows that some progress has been made against racism. But it should also be a reminder that much is left to be done.

Eric Hirsch
Assistant Professor of Sociology
Providence College

Bill Cosby receiving one of his many honorary degrees.

1

Thinking Big

On November 4, 1988, a group of two thousand people gathered in Atlanta, Georgia, to celebrate the inauguration of the new president of Spelman College. Among the many prominent people attending the event were two special guests: Bill Cosby and his wife, Camille.

Bill was dressed in a tuxedo, Camille in a long gown. Bill's face was serious, except when he turned to smile at his wife. And although there was no shortage of celebrities at the fundraiser, many eyes and cameras were turned in the direction of the table where Bill and Camille sat listening to the speeches and proceedings.

Spelman College had been founded more than one hundred years earlier, in 1881, as a private college dedicated to providing higher education for black women. The new president was Johnnetta B. Cole, the first black woman to hold that position.

It was no surprise that the Cosbys were present for the gala affair. The ties between the Cosby family and the venerable school were strong ones. One of Cosby's four daughters had attended Spelman. His hit television series, "The Cosby Show," had shot several episodes on the campus. Also, in the series, one of Cosby's TV daughters attended a college modeled on Spelman. Furthermore, Bill Cosby had known Cole for years. They had first met when Cosby was attending the University of Massachusetts and Cole was a professor of anthropology there.

Before the dinner ended that night, however, Bill Cosby and his wife would give Spelman College one of most delightful surprises in its history, setting an example for all who were concerned with the future of black education.

Standing in front of the large gathering, Johnnetta Cole spoke of the great work that had been accomplished in the first hundred years of Spelman's history. She also pointed out how much work remained and went on to say that the future of Spelman College, and of black colleges like it, depended on the generosity of people such as those in the room.

Much had indeed been accomplished in those hundred years. Spelman College had been born into an age of segregation in the South and had served as an important resource in the battle against prejudice and racism. Spelman had educated thousands of black women and had performed an important task in combatting ignorance and illiteracy. Even with the many changes that had occurred in the previous decades—the achievements of the civil rights movement and the subsequent improvement in education and employment opportunities for blacks—there was nevertheless a new generation of young black women growing up who very much needed schools like Spelman. Spelman College, Johnnetta Cole said, still had an important mission to perform.

Cole then announced that Bill and Camille Cosby had decided to donate $20 million to Spelman—the largest single gift ever given to a black college. The two thousand people at the dinner leaped to their feet; the room erupted in applause.

Bill Cosby walked up to the dais and, speaking for his wife and himself, said, "I want Johnnetta Cole to understand the love that Camille and I have for this college. The love we have for the women who, in spite of the odds against them, come to this school to challenge themselves, to challenge the school, then to challenge what we call the 'outside world.' "[1]

Cosby went on to explain why he had donated so much to Spelman: "Mrs. Cosby and I decided to stop black Americans and international black folk from across the ponds from thinking small. . . . I think we understand that these schools need money, but I think we've accepted that some white folk are going to either keep them alive or let them go."[2] By making this huge donation, Cosby suggested, it was time for blacks to shoulder more of the responsibility for educating black youth. It was time to start thinking big.

At that moment, Cosby knew better than anyone in America what it meant to think big, and to *be* big. The past year had been a record-shattering one for Cosby, a year in which he had become one of the best-paid and best-loved performers in the world. He had earned a staggering $57 million during that year—a phenomenal amount of money that broke down to more than $6,500 per hour, twenty-four hours each day. In addition to the success of "The Cosby Show" and his popularity as a nightclub performer, Cosby was also a best-selling author. *Fatherhood* had sold a record-breaking 2.6 million copies in hardcover, and *Time Flies* was selling so well that it threatened to break Cosby's own record. He also had a best-selling videocassette, *Bill Cosby: 49*. According to several independent surveys, Cosby had outrated, outsold, and outranked every other entertainer in history. He had achieved a record-high Q-score, which is the advertising industry's measure of audience appeal. Bill Cosby's popularity crossed all boundaries.

As Cosby returned to his table, there was more applause and more flashes from news photographers who were recording this historic event. Bill placed his hand on Camille's and listened to the other speakers. On his face was a serious, but pleased, expression.

People came over to congratulate him and thank him for his generosity to the school, but it was clear from their expressions that many did not know what to make of Bill Cosby. They were surprised to learn that he was as interested in education as he was in entertainment. Clearly he was a more complex person than they had imagined. As they left, they found that they had more questions than answers about who Bill Cosby was.

Who was this man whom millions of American families followed on television each week? Each Thursday night, at the end of "The Cosby Show" credits, the name William H. Cosby, Jr., Ed.D., appeared on the screen. Were the entertainer and the doctor of education the same person?

Who was this man whom most people felt comfortable calling "Cos?" Who was this black man who did not use racial humor to get a laugh? Cosby had begun working in the entertainment industry at a time when there were enormous barriers to black Americans. He had often been criticized by both blacks and whites who felt that his brand of gentle humor was an evasion, and that he should be more topical and race-oriented. Although he had used racial humor very early in his career, he had quickly abandoned it. Instead he chose to focus on that which unites people, not what separates them. This he considered a more universal language of humor, and the things he poked fun at were those that touched people of all backgrounds: childhood, marriage, family, the difficulties of raising children, and most recently, the effects of aging.

How comfortable was Bill Cosby with his phenomenal success? Cosby himself tended to play down his popularity. "I just go out there and do my job," he once told a magazine interviewer. "I'm not better than Eddie Murphy. I'm not better than Richard Pryor. I'm not better than Robin Williams. I'm not competing with anyone."[3]

Obviously he had mixed feelings about being a celebrity. He was especially concerned about his family being scrutinized by the public. Americans have always tended to raise celebrities to the ranks of near nobility. This worried Cosby, who once described his feelings about the fascination Americans have with the personal lives of celebrities: "I don't like it. My family and I just want to live. We want to deal with life without people coming up to us. When you're a celebrity, you don't want people coming up to your door, saying, 'You're on TV; we feel we own you.' "[4]

To protect their family from this public attention, Bill and Camille Cosby had made their 126 acre property in Amherst, Massachusetts, their primary home. There, away from the public eye, Bill and Camille raised their family.

Family life was important to Bill Cosby because of his deep commitment to basic family values. He had been married to the same woman, whom he had met on a blind date in 1962, for more than twenty-five years. On his wrist he wore a gold bracelet inscribed, "Camille's Husband."

Besides being a successful father and husband, Bill Cosby had, in the nearly thirty years he had been in show business, achieved extraordinary success in his chosen profession. He had become quite simply the most popular performer in television history. He was many things to many people: actor, comedian, father, singer, and writer. But the list did not define the man. The question remained: Who was the real Bill Cosby?

2

Life in Germantown

Even in the best of times, the Germantown section of Philadelphia was known as a poor, black neighborhood, and the 1930s were not the best of times. Instead, the 1930s saw the greatest economic depression in the history of the United States. At the height of the Great Depression, more than twenty-five percent of all Americans were out of work. Blacks especially had a difficult time finding work. Black neighborhoods like Germantown suffered terribly during these years.

It was into this environment that a son was born to Anna and William Cosby on July 12, 1937. The child was their first, and they named him William Henry Cosby, Jr.

Compared to the economic straits in which many of their neighbors found themselves, the Cosby family lived comfortably for a time. William Cosby, Sr., was a skilled welder and able to find work during these years. From the time Bill was born until late in 1943, the Cosby family lived in a small, two-story house on Beechwood Street. That house was the scene of many happy family gatherings. Sometimes more than twenty relatives would fill the house, celebrating and enjoying themselves. But this happy part of Bill Cosby's childhood did not last long.

Bill Cosby has said that the word father "still spells disappointment to my brothers and me."[1] Cosby's father was an intelligent but frustrated man who, according to his son, failed in life. Cosby once joked: "When I was a child, we kept moving down the economic ladder."[2] There was much truth behind this joke, as William Cosby, Sr., found it harder and harder to provide for his family. The 1940s and 1950s were a time when many obstacles, not of their own making, kept blacks from attaining economic success. Changes that would be brought about by the civil rights movement were still decades away, and William Cosby, Sr., faced a difficult struggle.

After Bill, three other sons were born to Anna and William; one of the sons, James, was often ill. There seemed to be no end to the bills that had to be paid. As a result, the pressure of having to make ends meet became

Cosby based many of his routines on his childhood.

too great for William Cosby, Sr. To escape his problems, he began to drink. The drinking, however, only made matters worse. He stayed out later each night, and more of his paycheck went toward alcohol. Finally, he lost his job, and the family was forced to move from the pleasant house on Beechwood Street to a series of small, cheerless apartments. One of the apartments, on Steward Street, had no bathtub. When someone needed to bathe, water had to be heated up on the stove in a large metal tub.

This was not a promising beginning, but it shows Bill Cosby's special genius for being able to extract laughter out of even the most painful periods of his childhood. Later, Cosby built a nightclub routine out of the way he took baths in the apartment on Steward Street. He told audiences that as a kid he had figured out an easier way of bathing. Heating up the water in a metal tub was too much trouble, he said, so he used to bathe in the toilet instead—and he'd warm up the water by dumping his brother in first.

Yet life with his father could not have been as funny as Bill later made it seem in his routines. The drinking problem of William Cosby, Sr., continued to worsen, and despite his skill as a welder he could hold down only odd jobs. As time went on, he contributed less and less to the support of his family, and sometimes he even beat his wife. The family finally ended up in a public housing project on Parish Street called the Richard Allen Homes. The Richard Allen Homes were among the first projects built for the poor in Philadelphia. Although plain and drab, they were not the worst place for a struggling family. There were many other families and children with whom Bill and his brothers could play.

During these years, and throughout Bill Cosby's childhood, there was one bright spark in his life: his mother, Anna. Anna Cosby sometimes said that the only thing she could give Bill and his brothers was love, and certainly there was plenty of that. Her love for her children helped to compensate for their father's failure.

Although Anna Cosby never took credit for Bill's success, she deserved much for the way she raised her children. She worked hard to instill in them a sense of right and wrong. She was strict with her sons but rarely hit them. Instead, when the boys did something wrong, her way of disciplining them was to cry. Cosby later said that he and his brothers found the sight of their mother's tears more painful than any physical punishment.

Anna Cosby set a positive example for her sons by her own actions, and she worked to provide a positive environment for them. Despite the fact that she was often busy and worried by the lack of money, she made certain to read to her children each night before they went to sleep. Sometimes she would read to them from the Bible, but other times she would read the stories of Mark Twain.

Mark Twain was the pen name of one of America's greatest writers, Samuel L. Clemens. Twain is most famous for his novels *Tom Sawyer* and *The Adventures of Huckleberry Finn,* but he also wrote humorous and satirical tales based on Bible stories. One is called "The Diary of Adam and Eve." In this story, Twain takes a comic look at the story of Adam and Eve. Bill and his brothers were very familiar with the Bible story, and Bill said that he found Mark Twain's version of it hilarious. The sharp, brisk wit made an impression on him, and later he would often acknowledge his debt to the humor of Mark Twain.

At the age of eight, however, Cosby experienced a painful loss: his younger brother, James, died. In 1945, James was stricken with rheumatic fever, an infectious disease that claimed the lives of many children before the use of penicillin and other antibiotics became widespread. James's death left a void in the family that could never be filled.

Meanwhile, William Cosby, Sr., finding it difficult to hold down a job in civilian life, decided to enlist in the navy. He became a steward on a navy ship, left the family at the Richard Allen Homes, and disappeared from their lives. For a while, he sent some money home, but it was never regular and never enough. Finally, it stopped coming altogether.

To feed and clothe her growing sons, Anna Cosby was forced to get work as a cleaning woman. She worked in the homes of white people, sometimes for twelve hours straight, and would return home, late at night, exhausted. And, despite all her efforts, she still could not make enough money to support the family. As a result, the Cosby family was forced to go on welfare—or, as it was known in the 1940s, relief. This cushion of money, arriving twice each month, was indeed a relief to Anna Cosby.

As the oldest child in the household, Bill felt the weight of responsibility on his shoulders. With his father gone, he had to help raise his brothers. This was a heavy load for a schoolboy to bear, but while his mother worked, Bill entertained and educated his younger brothers. He used the unselfish example of his mother to inspire him in setting an example for the younger boys.

Bill also tried to help with the household finances. From the age of nine, he always had a job of one kind or another. For a while, he shined shoes in downtown Philadelphia. After that, he sold fruit. One summer he worked in a local grocery store, stocking the shelves. This was a six-day-a-week job, and he worked from six in the morning until six at night, except on Saturdays when he worked until nine.

While the neighborhood where Bill grew up was not as rough as some inner-city neighborhoods are today, there were many wrong turns that a young teenager could take. Bill could have followed the example of some other children in his neighborhood who made their money by shoplifting. But whenever the temptation to do something wrong presented itself, he would think of his mother and of how hurt she would feel.

Despite Anna Cosby's hard work and Bill's jobs after school, there was never any money for even the smallest luxury or pleasure. This was expecially noticeable at Christmas time. Bill later remembered Christmas as the most difficult time of the year when he was growing up. The streets and store windows would be filled with lights and Christmas decorations. There would be Christmas trees in the houses and apartments of his friends. The other children in the neighborhood would be talking about the gifts they hoped to find under those trees. But in Bill's house, there were years when there wasn't even money for a tree, much less presents.

One year when his mother didn't have enough money to buy a Christmas tree, Bill decided that he would do something anyway to brighten up the house and lend it a Christmas spirit. So he painted an empty orange crate with bright colors and placed a tiny Santa Claus on top of it. When his mother came home and saw the "tree" that Bill had made, she cried. But these were not the tears of disappointment.

In spite of the fact that money was tight for the family, Anna felt that she had to do something special for Christmas. She went to some neighbors and borrowed money for a tree and some presents for the boys. Bill remembered that Christmas; he remembered how his mother sacrificed to bring the yuletide spirit to their apartment. And the memories of those Christmases in Philadelphia shaped his later attitude toward the holiday. As a grown man with his own family, he always tried to make Christmas a special time.

Despite the poverty of Bill's childhood, however, life in Germantown was not entirely grim. There was the great love and concern that Anna Cosby bore toward her children. And there was also a sense of unity and strength in the community. Everyone was in the same boat, struggling to succeed in the face of racial discrimination and economic hardship. As Bill grew older, he would draw on the strength and love of his mother, and on the support of people in his community, as he made his way into the world.

3

King Koko From Kookoo Island

Anna Cosby believed that people were judged as much by the style of their speech as by its content. She insisted that her children speak carefully, clearly, and in grammatically correct sentences. She did not want them to speak the way many people in the neighborhood spoke. Later, in a comedy routine that Cosby developed in nightclubs, he called his mother "the Person Who Enunciated and Hit You for Nothing."

Early on, Anna Cosby instilled a respect and a love for education in all of her children. It was on this strong foundation that Bill's career was later built. Bill was enrolled in the Wister Elementary School at age six. Although it was clear to many of his teachers that he was a bright child, it was equally clear that he was a lively, impatient one. He was often bored in class. There were probably many reasons for this.

For one, many of the subjects that were taught had little to do with his heritage. In the early 1940s, the teaching in most schools in the United States was rigid. Educators had a fixed notion of what constituted American history and world history, and it did not include blacks. History, as it was taught in schools around the nation, was a study of great men and important dates. The men, for the most part, were white. And the dates were ones that were important to white society. It would be more than thirty years before that would begin to change. Years would pass before the history of blacks was included in the history of the United States. Decades were to pass before the study of great men was to be broadened to include great men—and women—of many different races.

Wister Elementary could have provided important role models by having black teachers on the faculty. But Bill has recalled being taught by only two black teachers in all his school years. One time, one of the black teachers brought the class to an assembly program where all the students had to sing "Old Black Joe," a song about slavery. The children, unaware of the meaning of the lyrics, sang the song cheerfully and loudly. When the children returned to the classroom at the end of the assembly, however, the teacher began to cry. She feared that the children, without understanding the words of the song, were absorbing its message that blacks were not as good as whites. She made the children promise that they would never sing "Old Black Joe" again.

Bill was tall and popular with his classmates, who called him "Shorty" or "Cos." He excelled in sports and enjoyed telling jokes—sometimes more than he enjoyed listening to the teacher.

By the time he was in fifth grade, the school had placed him in a class for "problem students." Although his mother, who knew Bill was a bright child, was pained by this, it was actually to have a good effect on his life because he was to come into contact with a teacher who would leave a lasting impression on him.

Bill's fifth grade teacher was Mary Forchic. Forchic recognized that each of her students had something to offer the world and that each one was capable and deserving of an education. She also recognized that there might be circumstances preventing students from reaching their full potential, and she believed she could help.

Forchic tried to instill a sense of worth and value in each of her students. She guessed that many of them acted up in class because they craved attention, so she paid attention to them and gave them positive feedback. She tried to give them confidence in themselves. She wanted them to believe that they could be recognized for who they were without having to misbehave.

In Bill's case, Forchic recognized his athletic abilities and understood that this was an area in which he could excel. She encouraged him to pursue his interest in sports. She also encouraged him to entertain the other children in the class, and thereby transformed his desire for attention into a desire to perform. She gave him parts in school plays such as *King Koko from Kookoo Island, Back to the Simple Life,* and *Tom Tit Tot.* These plays were Bill's first opportunities to perform in public.

Bill performed his first comedy routine in the sixth grade. Mary Forchic caught him doing it during class, but she thought it was so funny that, to his surprise, she asked him to repeat it so the whole class could hear. Later, in high school, he continued to use his quick wit and humor. Once a teacher caught him reading a comic book during class and confiscated it. He told Bill that he could get the comic book back at the end of the school year. Bill quickly shot back: "Why? Does it take you that long to read it?"[1]

Fortunately for Bill, Forchic also believed that the duties of a teacher do not end at the classroom door. She believed that it was important to expand her students' idea of the world and to let them know what was beyond the boundaries of their neighborhood. Once Forchic treated Bill to a movie and dinner afterwards. This gave Bill a tremendous feeling of self-esteem, a feeling he never forgot. "I was so happy to be downtown," he later said of the experience. "After the movie, my teacher took me to dinner and then she drove me home in a taxicab. This was a big thing, because in my neighborhood if you rode in a taxicab something bad or something wonderful had happened to you."[2]

Forchic was Bill's teacher in the fifth and sixth grades. During the first year, Bill showed little improvement, still playing the role of class clown. But in the second year, he began to change. He became the captain of the baseball and track teams, and he was elected president of his class. His grades improved, too. Forchic wrote on his report card: "William is a boy's boy, an all-around fellow, and he should grow up to do some great things."[3] Years later, Bill looked back gratefully at the encouragement and support that Forchic had given him.

After sixth grade, Bill entered Fitzsimons Junior High School. It was an awkward, difficult age for him. At Fitzsimons, there were fewer black students than white students, and Bill saw the different values that each culture had. In addition, he was entering adolescence and becoming interested in girls. At the same time, his status was also becoming clear to him. The girls he was interested in wanted to go out with boys who dressed nicely and who had money to treat them. But Bill was poor. He had no money to go out on dates with girls he liked. On the night of the junior-high prom, he went to pick up his date but had no money for a cab. Fortunately for him, the girl's parents gave him money for a cab so that he could arrive at the prom in style.

In his final year at junior high, Bill took an IQ test and scored so high that he was placed in a gifted program at Central High School. It was a great opportunity for him. The brightest students in Philadelphia attended Central. The school boasted a football team on which the players wore real uniforms, were well-coached, and played a regular schedule of games against other high schools in the city.

But Bill was not able to take advantage of all the opportunities that Central High School had to offer. He faced several handicaps. For one thing, the school's student body was overwhelmingly white and he felt out of place. He was one of the few black students at Central from the Germantown neighborhood. A second problem was that Bill lacked good study habits. Students at Central studied hard. But Bill, used to coasting on his native intelligence, could not keep up.

It seemed that sports were his only outlet for self-expression at Central, but even in this he was handicapped. He broke his arm during the first week of football practice and was out for the season. After his arm healed, he tried out for the baseball and track teams. But he did not excel at either sport while he was at Central.

Instead, Bill began to suffer from a case of the blues. At Central , he was quiet and hardly clowned at all. He missed his old friends, and spent the days at Central waiting for the bell to ring so that he could rejoin the gang at the Richard Allen Projects. There, among his friends, he clowned around and felt good about himself and his abilities. Everybody in his gang told jokes to see who could come up with the funniest ones, but Bill Cosby always won.

Some of his material Bill got from watching comedians on television. One of the kids in the neighborhood had a TV, and all the other kids would parade into his house to watch the comedy shows. The favorite shows featured Jack Benny, George Burns, and George Gobel. Bill loved "Your Show of Shows," which starred Sid Caesar and Imogene Coca and had some of the funniest material. When his family was finally able to afford a TV set, Bill was overjoyed. He would spend hours watching the comedies, studying the timing of the comedians on the shows.

In later years, Cosby often returned to Germantown.

After his freshman year at Central, Bill transferred to Germantown High School, where he could be with his friends. All the same, his academic performance did not improve, and at the end of his sophomore year he was told that he was being held back. He would have to repeat the year. Bill didn't want to be the oldest kid in his class and be known as the boy who'd been held back. So, rather than repeat the grade, he dropped out of high school altogether.

Anna Cosby was very upset by her son's decision. Although there might be jobs available, she knew that for a black man without an education, things would be bleak indeed. But Bill had not forgotten the values that she had tried to instill in him as a child. He hadn't given up. And he hadn't forgotten Mary Forchic's prediction that he would grow up to do some great things. While he wasn't exactly sure how to go about doing it, he meant to make that prediction come true.

4

In the Navy

After dropping out of Germantown High School, Cosby treaded water for a while. He decided to look for work, telling his mother that he wanted to contribute more to the household finances. The kind of job did not matter to him. The most important thing, he said later, was to keep himself busy and keep himself off the streets, where the temptation existed to turn to robbery. He had seen some of his neighbors turn to crime to support themselves, and he did not want to find himself in that desperate position.

While jobs for high shool dropouts were available, most of them led nowhere. Cosby's first job after dropping out of school was in a shoe-repair shop. But he quickly tiring of the dull work there and began putting women's heels on men's shoes to amuse himself. The owner of the shop, however, was not amused, and Cosby left the job soon afterward.

His next job was working in a car muffler plant—a job almost as boring as shoe repair. It became clear to Cosby that the jobs available to a black man without a basic education were boring and repetitious and paid poorly. At this rate, Cosby knew, he would never be able to find work that engaged his mind and his talents. He would never be able to improve himself and the position of his mother and brothers by simply going from one low-paying job to another.

Seeing that many other young men in the neighborhood were enlisting in the armed forces, Cosby decided to look into it. Perhaps by joining one of the services, he could improve his options. Perhaps spending time away from the streets could broaden his view of life.

In 1956, following in the footsteps of his father, Cosby joined the navy and became a hospital corpsman. He was trained in various medical techniques, including physical therapy. The navy promised young recruits a chance to see the world but Cosby spent most of his tour of duty in the United States, at the marine base at Quantico, Virginia, and at Bethesda Naval Hospital in Maryland. He did, however, sail on ships bound for Newfoundland and Guantanamo Bay, Cuba.

The United States was not at war when Cosby enlisted, and his work consisted mostly of physical therapy sessions with navy and marine veterans who had been and disabled during the Korean War. He enjoyed working with the vets. He helped them exercise arms and legs rendered useless by wounds. Although it was painful at times to work with the severely disabled, Cosby liked the close contact with people.

He was a popular fellow in the hospital wards because he liked to tell jokes and cheer people up. He was also popular because of his athletic abilities. Cosby joined the navy's track team and won awards in meets against teams from the other services. He took part in the national Amateur Athletic Union competitions, pitting himself against the finest amateur athletes from all over the United States. At one of these, Cosby managed to high-jump six feet five inches, placing seventeenth in a field that included the best high jumpers in the nation.

During some of the meets, however, Cosby struggled against not only his competition but also the ugliness of racism. The armed forces had been integrated in 1948 by President Harry S. Truman, but the United States was still a deeply segregated nation. Things were only beginning to change. In 1954, lawyers for the National Association for the Advancement of Colored People (NAACP) won a historic victory when the Supreme Court ruled in the case of *Brown* v. *Board of Education* that segregated public schools were unconstitutional. This decision led to the challenging of other laws designed to keep blacks segregated from the rest of society.

The next great step toward civil rights for blacks was taken in 1955 when Rosa Parks, a seamstress in Montgomery, Alabama, refused to give up her seat on a bus to a white man. And because Montgomery city law required blacks to sit or stand in the backs of city buses, Parks was arrested. At that time, Martin Luther King, Jr., was the pastor of the Dexter Avenue Baptist Church in Montgomery. In response to Parks's arrest, he organized a mass boycott of the bus system by blacks. Lasting more than a year, the Montgomery bus boycott succeeded in forcing the city to repeal its discriminatory law. With that victory, the civil rights movement discovered both King and the power of his philosophy of nonviolent civil disobedience.

But the civil rights movement's greatest victories were still far off while Cosby was in the navy. When his track-and-field team traveled to military bases in the Deep South, Cosby knew that he would be faced with segregated conditions. Whites and blacks were still not allowed to eat together in the South, and some places had separate counters where blacks had to take their meals. Still others refused to serve "coloreds." Often, as the rest of the team entered through the front door, Cosby was forced to go to the back of a restaurant to be served.

One of Cosby's reasons for going into the navy was to give himself time to sort things out in his life, and he did gain maturity there. He suspected that he had more brains and ability than most of the other men in his outfit, but it took him time to realize that it was foolish to waste his time goofing off when he could be gaining skills that would help him after he left the service. He signed up for a special course to complete his high school education, did well, and received his degree. But he had no intention of settling for only a high school degree. He had bigger plans than that.

Cosby didn't want to return to civilian life and go back to his old routine of being supported by his mother. Instead, he decided he would go to college, major in physical education, and become a teacher. That way, Cosby could help young black children. He remembered how important his own teacher, Mary Forchic, had been in shaping his ideas and self-image.

When he got out of the navy, Cosby applied for an athletic scholarship to Temple University in Philadelphia, so he could be close to his family while studying. Temple was quick to grant him a scholarship. Besides being impressed with his grades in the navy courses and his athletic abilities, the school officials were also influenced by his attitude. Cosby had come out of the navy a determined and serious man. Ernie Casale, Temple's athletic director while Cosby was there, recalled that, rather than just socializing, Cosby remained interested in obtaining his degree and being a good athlete. In the years that he'd wasted between dropping out of high school and joining the navy, he had glimpsed what the future might hold for a black man with no academic credentials. It had scared and motivated him. Bill Cosby didn't want to end up in a factory or a shoe-repair shop.

At Temple, he tried out for the football, basketball, and track teams. On the football team, he earned a spot as a fullback, but just as at Central, an injury prevented him from playing. He sat out most of his freshman season with a broken collarbone.

Still, Cosby enjoyed his first year at Temple. He was popular with his classmates, even though he didn't live on campus. His years in the navy had helped him develop social skills. In the navy, he had met people of all races and from all different walks of life, and he had learned to be comfortable around them. He was no longer intimidated by, or ill at ease with, whites, and his easygoing manner and sense of humor were a great help in dealing with people. He knew that he could make people laugh, and he knew that people laughed because they liked him.

As Cosby finished his freshman year, a new decade was beginning—the 1960s. It was also the start of a new era in race relations in the United States. Over the next few years, blacks would march, demonstrate, and protest to bring about great changes in civil rights. The wall of segregation was about to fall.

Cosby was aware of all this, but he didn't actively participate. He was busy studying and playing sports. His contributions to race relations were still some years away, and were to take a more unusual form.

5

Starting at the Cellar

At the end of Cosby's freshman year, he went to California. He had hoped to work there during the summer. But when he tried to find work, he discovered that all the doors he wanted to open were shut to him because of the color of his skin. It was a frustrating time. As Cosby recalled, "I got so tired of riding buses and spending money to hear some guy say 'Well. . . .' Finally I just called and said over the phone, 'Do you hire Negroes?' 'No.' I wasn't Bill Cosby, famous entertainer, then. I was just a black man trying to get work. . . . [T]he door was being locked. And it was unfair."[1]

When Cosby returned to Temple in the fall, he was the second-string fullback on the football team. Although he later said that he was never a very good football player, those who remember his playing days disagree, saying that he might have made it to the pros. The New York Giants scouted him during his sophomore season. But Bill Cosby was not headed toward a career in football because that year something happened that would shape his future. It changed things so that he could never go back to his dreams of becoming a physical education teacher. In fact, the only phys ed teaching he would ever do would be as a character on a television program.

Although Cosby was attending Temple on an athletic scholarship, he needed pocket money, and so he decided to take a part-time job tending bar at a place in downtown

Philadelphia called the Cellar. He mixed drinks and tried to keep a loose and relaxed atmosphere in the bar by telling jokes. Soon he had his customers rolling in the aisles.

He still watched comedians on television, but now he would write down their funniest lines and use them on his customers. Comedy record albums were also becoming very popular, and Cosby picked up material from albums by such comedians as Mort Sahl and Orson Bean. And finally he even began to use some of his own jokes. Soon he was spending less time tending bar and more time doing routines.

Mort Sahl

Cosby got such good response from the patrons of the Cellar that the manager of the bar realized he had a real talent on his hands. The manager also ran a nightclub in the same building, called the Underground, where he booked musical acts and comedians. He offered Cosby a job there, telling jokes to warm the audience up before the main act, for five dollars a night.

Many amateurs can be funny in friendly, informal settings but freeze once they're placed under a spotlight in front of strangers. They forget their timing and their lines and become self-conscious about what they're doing. This was true even of some of America's most famous comedians. When Woody Allen first started out as a co-median, he used to stand with his back to the audience and tell jokes. He was terrified by a live audience.

Woody Allen

The Underground gave Cosby his first experience on stage before a live audience. To his surprise, he found himself completely at ease. He had always enjoyed performing and being the center of attention. The audiences at the Underground laughed at his jokes, and the older comedians, for whom he warmed up the crowd, also found him funny. Once in a while the featured comedian would not appear, and the manager would let Cosby fill in. Cosby began by telling stories about campus life at Temple, and his act improved with each show.

Soon, Cosby got work at other clubs in the Philadelphia area and found that wherever he went, audiences responded to his humor. About this time, a cousin of his became the first black to host a television show in Philadelphia, and he gave Cosby a chance to do the audience warm-up. And the audiences for the television show laughed as hard as the Cellar audiences had.

Cosby found that he was enjoying his routines as much as the audiences were, and slowly the idea of a comedy career formed in his mind. He realized that he might be able to do stand-up comedy for a living. The money wasn't bad—sometimes he earned as much as $20 a night—and it was possible for an ambitious comedian to earn a great deal more. Television variety shows and situation comedies had created many openings. And there was the standard nightclub and resort circuit. The more Cosby thought about it, the more the idea of a career in comedy appealed to him.

The popularity of stand-up comedy seems to come in cycles, and as Cosby was starting out, a new cycle was beginning. A new generation of stand-up comedians was breaking into show business, and comedy clubs were

Dick Gregory

sprouting up all across the country. The audiences, too, were becoming more open to different kinds of humor. They laughed at the old Bob Hope-type one-liners, but also enjoyed hip humor, political humor, and ethnic humor.

Moreover, white audiences were finally willing to listen to young black comedians. Until this time, black comedians had mostly entertained black audiences. When they entertained whites, it was mainly by playing degrading racial stereotypes. But now white audiences were anxious to listen to the sharp, quick wit of black comedians like Dick Gregory and Godfrey Cambridge, whose racial and political humor was both funny and relevant to the problems and situations of the times.

As the laughter he was creating at the Underground and other Philadelphia clubs grew, Cosby realized that it was time to expand his horizons and try his routines elsewhere. It was time to go to New York.

"Cos" in his Greenwich Village days.

6

Stand-Up

As Bill Cosby drove from Philadelphia to New York City in 1962 to try his luck at the clubs in Greenwich Village, things were changing rapidly in the United States. A new, young president, John F. Kennedy, was in the White House. The winds of change were blowing. The civil rights movement was in full swing, and leaders such as Martin Luther King, Jr., and Malcolm X were demanding equal rights for all Americans. People were listening. And in the field of entertainment, new, younger audiences were searching out unusual and more out-spoken forms of amusement.

Stand-up comedy in the early 1960s reflected much of the turbulence the nation was undergoing. New come-dians, whose humor was more suited to the times, were taking the place of the older, more established comedians who had dominated the comedy landscape since the 1940s.

It has often been said that comedy is no laughing matter. If that's true, then the most deadly serious form of comedy is stand-up. Stand-up is more than the act of delivering sixty jokes over a period of fifteen minutes and making people laugh every fifteen seconds. Instead, the stand-up comedian fulfills the necessary role of inspired madman, creating laughter while he simultaneously pre-sents material that is thought-provoking and sometimes cutting. It has often been pointed out that many serious points are better made with humor than in earnest. The comedian is allowed to say things about society that people are too afraid to say directly.

Comedians have played a special social role since ancient times. In the royal courts of medieval Europe, for example, fools entertained the kings and queens, saying things for which other people might have been beheaded. They were not only skillful performers, but also keen observers of their societies.

The modern era of humor in the United States was born in the vaudeville theaters that sprang up in every city in the late nineteenth century. Vaudeville shows like the Ziegfeld Follies offered a variety of entertainment, and nearly all included comedians who delivered rapid-fire jokes. Theirs was a fast, hard, unsentimental brand of humor—an urban humor, a slick humor of the streets. Great comedians such as Bob Hope, Mae West, Sophie Tucker, and teams like George Burns and Gracie Allen, came out of the vaudeville era. Many went into the new media of film, records, and radio. Charlie Chaplin, Buster Keaton, and Laurel and Hardy made countless films in the early days of Hollywood. Fred Allen, Bob Hope, and Jack Benny were popular radio comedians. Records with funny songs were popular, too. Bert Williams was the first black comedian to be recorded.

In the late 1950s and early 1960s, however, audiences changed, and the comedians did, too. Up until that time, comedy routines had been straightforward. Stand-up comedians such as Red Skelton and Milton Berle relied on one-liners that were formal and quick. But the stand-up comedians who emerged in the late 1950s rejected that older kind of comedy. The leaders of this "new wave" of

Bert Williams

comedy—Lenny Bruce, Mort Sahl, and Dick Gregory—were cynical, intellectual, sophisticated, and combative. Attacking all of the institutions of society, their humor covered politics, sex, and social commentary. It was shocking, and it was meant to shock.

Audiences packed the small coffeehouses and nightclubs where these new comedians performed along with folk musicians, jazz musicians, and beatnik poets. Audiences expected the songs to be protest songs; they expected the jazz to be free and improvisational; they expected the poetry to be complicated; and they expected the comedians to be outrageous.

The most important young comedian of the time was Lenny Bruce, a Jew who had grown up in New York. In his comedy routines, he used profanity and ethnic phrases to shock his audiences into self-awareness. No group was immune to his sharp wit, which influenced most of the other comedians coming up.

"Moms" Mabley

Redd Foxx

Until the early 1960s, the young, white coffeehouse audience did not know what to expect from black stand-up comedians. Segregation in the entertainment field had denied black comedians access to white audiences, so before 1960 few whites knew of black comedians such as "Moms" Mabley, Slappy White, Redd Foxx, and George Kirby. And even those few black comedians who had been able to gain some exposure had two sets of jokes—one for white audiences, the other for black audiences. Like much of black life, black humor remained invisible to white people. In the minds of many whites, blacks were the objects of humor rather than the creators of it. As a result, white audiences were not aware of the depth and richness of black humor.

But the great changes of the 1960s thrust black comedians before the larger, white American public. And once on this stage, black comedians were able to use humor to tell the hard truth about race relations in a way that whites found acceptable. Addressing white audiences, Dick Gregory told a story about a black man going into a restaurant. The owner says, "We don't serve Nigras!" "That's cool," says the black man. "I don't eat them."[1] Redd Foxx was more threatening. When an audience didn't laugh at his jokes, Foxx would say, "Why should I be wasting my time with you here when I could be knifing you in an alley?"[2] Foxx also joked that the first black to receive an athletic scholarship from the University of Mississippi was a javelin catcher.

Thus white audiences at Greenwich Village comedy clubs such as the Bitter End came to expect subversive humor from black comedians—a hip humor that was bitter, angry, and racial. In short, they came to expect Dick Gregory knockoffs. But in 1962, a new talent arrived in New York who didn't perform as expected.

7

The Village

In 1962, New York was *the* place to be for young comics, offering opportunties that were unavailable in Philadelphia. One area of opportunity was television. Today, most television shows are filmed in Los Angeles. But in 1962, many variety shows were still being produced in New York. These shows—such as Ed Sullivan's "Toast of the Town," "The Danny Kaye Show," and "The Tonight Show"—often provided a showcase for young comedians. Talent scouts for these shows would scour the small comedy clubs in Greenwich Village, searching for new and fresh talent.

Competition was fierce at the clubs, but Bill Cosby was able to take it on and succeed. Once he had competed against his neighborhood friends to make people laugh; now he did the same thing on a larger scale. But would he be the funniest?

Cosby arrived from Philadelphia with a list of comedy clubs in the Village. And because the neighborhood had always attracted off-beat, intelligent, artistic types, Cosby fit in well. He auditioned at a few clubs and was finally hired by Clarence Hood, who ran the Gaslight, a tiny club in the basement of a small building. In addition to comedians, Hood also booked a wide array of musical talent.

From the start, Cosby's originality was immediately apparent to anyone who heard him. In those early days, however, people were more impressed by his style and personality than by material, which was often racial. (In one routine, Cosby talked about being the first black president of the United States. He tells a friend, "Yeah, baby, everything's fine, except a lot of 'For Sale' signs are going up on this block."[1]) But as many comedians have noted, the trick is not to say funny things, but to say things funny. And Bill Cosby knew just how to do that.

Soon everybody was talking about the black comedian at the Gaslight, and more people began to show up for Cosby's shows. Hood started him off at a salary of $60 per week plus a free room over the club. But once Cosby proved his popularity, Hood extended Cosby's gig indefinitely and doubled his salary. The *New York Times* even ran an enthusiastic piece about Cosby, headlined "Philadelphia Negro Aims His Barbs at Race Relations." The writer of the article praised Cosby and mentioned that he was still attending Temple, where he was on the football and track teams.

These were exciting times to be young, talented, and living in Greenwich Village. The year 1962 was an important year for folk music, and the Village was its mecca. Bob Dylan was playing such venues as the Gaslight, the Bitter End, and Folk City. Simon and Garfunkel were also playing the same clubs. And two native New Yorkers, both one-time comedy writers, were now pursuing performing careers instead. Their names were Woody Allen and Joan Rivers.

The young comedians were struggling to sharpen their acts. Some of them learned from television, some from each other, but they all learned from Lenny Bruce. Speaking about Lenny Bruce, Cosby said:

Lenny Bruce

I remember being very upset that people would come in to see Lenny knowing that he was going to use four-letter words. At that time in the sixties . . . that was really taboo. And I'm sitting in the Village Vanguard—I went to see Lenny because I had all of his records, and the cuts that I enjoyed the most had to do with human behavior—and I'll be darned. Lenny started talking, and in the dialogue of the way the people talked, Lenny used a four-letter word. And four people, as if they had been rehearsing this, stood up and said out loud, "I've never heard such language in my life."

And I remember being very, very angry with these people.[2]

Cosby learned many things from Lenny Bruce. But there was one thing that he decided not to learn, which was Bruce's style of engagement. Bruce often battled with people in the audience who, like those Cosby remembered, would come to his shows just waiting for Bruce to say something outrageous, so that they could stand up and leave. Bruce would get angry and frustrated with these people, and often some very serious humor would come out of those moments.

Cosby could see that this behavior was not his style. There were times performing at the Gaslight when he'd become angry with audiences who were not getting the humor. But he never fought the audience. He kept his feelings under tight control and just accepted those shows that did not go over well. He learned to endure the terrible sound of silence that filled a room after a one-liner or a story missed the mark.

By this time, Cosby had picked up a manager, Roy Silver, to help him arrange bookings and work on his act. It was Silver who told Cosby to drop the racial material from his routines, insisting that Cosby was merely doing publicity for Dick Gregory. So Cosby dropped the racial jokes and began to draw on more personal material: Philadelphia, football, and growing up. He began to realize that while he admired the routines of Gregory and others, and respected their criticisms of racial discrimination, he didn't therefore have to adopt their approach to comedy. Cosby had his own unique style and way of expressing himself, and in time he would find his own way of addressing race relations.

Cosby had very few routines at this time, and it was clear to him and to Silver that he would need to develop more. At each of Cosby's shows, Silver would sit in the audience with a tape recorder. At the end of the night, they would go upstairs to Cosby's room above the Gaslight or to Silver's apartment, and there they would play back the recording of the show, listening to the jokes and trying to figure out why some had succeeded and others had failed. In one show a joke would work, while in another it would flop. Was it the audience? Had Cosby's delivery and timing been off? They analyzed each joke and each pause until Cosby began to find his own comic timing and voice. By the end of the summer, Cosby's act was coming together. Several chances to appear on a television variety show had not panned out. But while he hadn't gotten his big career break, he was getting better gigs, becoming more and more accomplished on stage, and gaining more and more confidence in himself.

After the summer in New York, Cosby returned to Temple to attend classes and rejoin the football team. But as the fall months dragged on, he felt himself caught between two conflicting desires. He wanted to complete his degree, becoming the first member of his family to graduate from college. But the applause and excitement of being a comedian kept calling him.

That fall, Cosby tried to do both things—go to college and continue performing. On weekdays, he attended classes. On weeknights, he did his homework and worked on new comedy material. On weekend days, he played fullback on the Temple football team. And on weekend nights, he performed his routine wherever Roy Silver managed to book him.

This schedule was much too hectic, however, and something had to give. The moment of truth came one day when the football team had to travel overnight to Toledo for a Saturday game. The problem was that Cosby also had a show to do that Friday night. He didn't want to break the engagement; he would be paid more than $200 for a couple of hours of work. Cosby told the coach that he would go to Toledo the next morning.

The coach, George Makris, and Ernie Casale, the athletic director, wanted to be fair and accommodating to Cosby. They knew that doing comedy was important to him. But they also knew that it was unfair to the team to give any individual special treatment. And they felt that Cosby was trying to do too much at once.

Casale told Cosby that if he wanted to stay with the team, he had to make the trip to Toledo with them. Casale later recalled that Cosby smiled when faced with the choice, as if he'd been waiting for this chance to decide.

Cosby's mother, Anna, was very unhappy when he told her that he was dropping out of Temple in favor of a career in comedy. She simply couldn't understand how he could leave college for the risky world of show business. She knew that only a handful of performers succeed in making a decent living, while a college graduate with a degree in physical education would have solid employment opportunities. Despite all his arguments, Bill Cosby could not convince his mother that he was doing the right thing.

8

The Tonight Show

The period between the fall of 1962 and winter of 1963 was the longest and most tense in Bill Cosby's life. He was struggling to prove to himself—and to the people around him—that he'd made the right decision about leaving college. He worked whenever and wherever Roy Silver got him a booking, playing all over the Northeast in the various comedy clubs that made up the circuit for new talent. In a good week, he would make several hundred dollars; in a bad week, next to nothing.

But he was beginning to build a reputation as a talented black comedian whose routines did not depend on racial jokes for laughs. To be sure, there were nights when the audience refused to listen to his tales of growing up in Philadelphia; there were nights when the audiences expected and wanted racial humor. But he didn't lose heart. On those nights, Cosby accomodated the audiences, but he slipped in his stories between the racial jokes. He continued to develop his material and spin his Mark Twain-inspired tales of childhood. Cosby had a vision, and he intended to follow that vision to its logical conclusion. He would be his own man.

The first months of 1963 were an important time. Although the breakthrough of a television booking continued to elude him, plans were in the works for a comedy album. Roy Silver knew an executive at Warner Brothers Records who owed him a favor. Besides, comedy albums were hot, and every record label was scrambling to sign up new talent. Silver was able to convince his friend that Cosby was going to make it big.

Nineteen sixty-three was also an important year for Cosby in other ways. It was in that year that he met the woman he would marry—Camille Hanks.

A friend of Cosby's had been trying to match him up with Camille for quite some time, but Cosby had been too busy, rushing from one club date to another. Finally, after returning from a show that he did in Washington, D.C., Cosby went out on a date with her. She was nineteen at the time, and a psychology major at the University of Maryland.

The two came from very different backgrounds. Hanks had grown up in Silver Spring, Maryland, a middle-class suburb far from the tough streets of North Philadelphia. Her father was a chemistry researcher at the Walter Reed Army Hospital. She was reluctant to go out with Cosby, but once they met they hit it off. Two weeks later, Cosby asked Hanks to marry him. A few months later, she said yes.

Her parents, however, would not hear of their daughter marrying a comedian. Show business people had a reputation for unreliability. What kind of family life could she expect from a man whose business required so much travel? They made Camille break off the engagement.

Yet Cosby stood firm. Hanks's parents could force her to break off their engagement, but they couldn't keep him from seeing her. He continued to date her, believing that once her parents got to know him, they would like him, too.

In the year that had passed since the summer of 1962, an extraordinary number of things had happened to Cosby. He'd left college. He'd begun to establish himself as a comedian. And he met the woman of his dreams. But there was one thing missing—the television appearance. Cosby and Silver both knew that such an appearance, particularly on an important variety show, was the difference between success and failure.

Then, in the sumer of 1963, a call came from "The Tonight Show," inviting Cosby to come in for an audition. Johnny Carson, the regular host of the show, had taken a week off from work, and the guest host was Allan Sherman, who had become a sensation overnight with the album *My Son the Folksinger.*

Because Cosby had auditioned many times before for "The Tonight Show," each time with no success, he almost turned down the offer, not wanting to have to deal with the pain of another disappointment. But he quickly thought better of it, and took a cab uptown to the NBC building where "The Tonight Show" was taped. At the studio, Sherman asked him to perform the routine he intended to use on the show. Cosby did as he was told, but Sherman just looked on blankly, without laughing. Then, unexpectedly, Sherman told him to get ready for the show.

That night Cosby did one of his best routines. It had to do with karate schools, which were very popular in those days. Late-night television was full of commercials promising to turn weaklings into fearless fighting machines. Cosby's routine was about a man who had just graduated from a karate school and whose hand was so calloused that it looked like a foot. "Keep your hand in your pocket for nine days," Cosby's advice went. "Then, when someone attacks you, you take a swing at them and even if you miss, the smell'll kill them."[1]

Cosby had performed the routine countless times before, in small clubs all over the Northeast, but he was not prepared for the response he got from the "Tonight Show" audience. People screamed with laughter as he told how someone with the correct karate shout could frighten robbers into giving themselves up.

After his "Tonight Show" appearance, Cosby's nightclub fees skyrocketed. He was making upwards of $700 a week, and suddenly Warner Brothers was eager to push his record, *Bill Cosby Is a Very Funny Fellow . . . Right!,* which was recorded live at the Bitter End and produced by Roy Silver and Allan Sherman. Although the record did not sell well, Bill Cosby was on his way.

Cosby on "The Tonight Show."

Cosby with his wife, Camille.

Finally, in January 1964, Cosby and Hanks were married. In addition to spending the past year working on his career, he had also been trying hard to make a good impression on Hanks's parents. At last, he succeeded. They decided to forgive Cosby for being a comedian and allowed him to marry their daughter. Bill and Camille Cosby spent their honeymoon crisscrossing the United States—Cosby was booked solid at various comedy clubs. Things were looking up. Money was coming in and Cosby was getting more television appearances.

But Bill Cosby's life was about to change in a way that he could never have imagined.

In his "I Spy" dressing room.

9

Television's Jackie Robinson

After a show at the Crescendo in early 1965, a man came backstage to congratulate Cosby and tell him how much he admired his work. The man was Carl Reiner, a well-known comedian and writer. He had worked on a successful television variety series called "Your Show of Shows," for which he and Mel Brooks had created many famous routines. Reiner would go on to direct and write many film comedies, but at that time he was still working in television as a co-producer of the "The Dick Van Dyke Show."

Cosby had admired Reiner for many years. "Your Show of Shows" had been one of his favorite programs, and one of the routines that Reiner and Brooks had created, "The Two-Thousand-Year-Old Man," had inspired Cosby to develop "Noah and the Ark," one of his most famous routines. Reiner's praise meant a lot to Cosby. But Reiner hadn't come backstage simply to pay Cosby a compliment; he also told Cosby that a television producer by the name of Sheldon Leonard very much wanted to see him.

Leonard was one of the most successful and innovative producers of the time, as well as Reiner's co-producer on "The Dick Van Dyke Show." He was known for having a good eye for talent and being a risk-taker. One of the risks he had taken early on in "The Dick Van Dyke Show" was to do an episode in which Van Dyke believes that his newborn baby has been mistakenly switched for another baby. Dick Van Dyke calls the parents of the other baby; when they come to his house, they turn out to be black.

The television network and the show's sponsor had been worried about the episode. Were television audiences ready for interracial jokes? But Leonard had been stubborn. He'd insisted that the show would work and that if it wasn't acceptable to the live audience, he would reshoot the episode using a white couple. Leonard had been proved right by the audience's laughter and the ratings of the episode.

Cosby and his manager, Roy Silver, knew of Leonard. They assumed that he wanted to offer Cosby a guest role on the Van Dyke show. As it turned out, Sheldon Leonard did have a role in mind for Cosby, but it wasn't as a guest on a comedy show. Leonard wanted Cosby to star in a new dramatic series.

Leonard had seen Cosby do some of his routines on television and had admired his abilities. He had a feeling that Cosby could be a good actor as well as a good comedian, and that he might be right for a spy drama that Leonard was developing for NBC. "I Spy" chronicled the ongoing adventures of two CIA agents who traveled around the world posing as a tennis player and his trainer. The tennis player was to be played a white actor, Robert Culp, but the role of the trainer was still unfilled.

During the mid-1960s, spy movies were on almost every movie screen in the country. The James Bond movie, *Dr. No*, had been so successful that many copycat movies followed. Now television was getting into the act, too, with Leonard leading the way. He wanted "I Spy"

On the set of "I Spy" with costar Robert Culp.

to be special. Each episode would have a huge budget, and the show would be shot on locations all over the globe rather than on a Hollywood back lot. And as though this were not enough to set "I Spy" apart, Leonard wanted Bill Cosby to play the role of the trainer, making "I Spy" the first show in television history on which a black would have equal billing with a white. What's more, Cosby's character would be an Oxford-educated Rhodes scholar, so he would be the "brains" of the duo.

Bill Cosby agreed to do the show.

Everyone understood that a lot was riding on Cosby's casting. NBC was especially nervous that southern stations might refuse to carry the show, and that some advertisers would pull their commericals rather than have their products associated with a controversial program. A final problem was that Cosby had no professional acting experience. In fact, he hadn't acted since *King Koko From Kookoo Island.*

Leonard knew that he was taking a risk, but it was a calculated risk nonetheless. If the show was good, and if the chemistry was right between the two stars, then "I Spy" could become a huge hit and bring a major change in television programming.

As the first episodes went into production, the pressure on Cosby was intense. *Variety,* the newspaper of the film and television industry, had dubbed him "Television's Jackie Robinson." At times, it seemed as though every reporter in the world was showing up to ask him the same questions about integration. In the meatime, he still had to learn the art of television acting. He was used to playing before live audiences, not in front of the cold eye of the camera. He was used to writing his own lines and creating his own characters, not delivering lines written by others. Many times he messed up his lines or didn't follow stage directions. At other times, the camera and the technicians made him self-conscious, and his lines came out stiff and forced.

But Cosby had a number of things going for him. First, there was Sheldon Leonard's confidence in him. Second, there was the support of his costar, Robert Culp. Culp worked closely with Cosby, giving him pointers on acting. The two men developed a strong friendship off-screen, which came across on-screen as well. Third, there was the support he got from his family. Cosby knew that he had to succeed because the issue of integration was much larger than his career. It involved future opportunities for black actors and entertainers. He was breaking new ground, and a great deal depended on him.

Once "I Spy" aired in the fall of 1965, however, the show was an instant success. Surveys done by various rating services demonstrated that it had broad appeal. Viewers believed in the friendship between the white tennis star and the black trainer. They accepted the show's premise that a black man could be equal to a white man in every way. The surveys also showed that people responded to Bill Cosby's acting and character. More than two hundred television stations around the country aired the show. Only four stations in the South refused to broadcast it. NBC was greatly relieved.

At the end of the season, Cosby received an Emmy award for his role in "I Spy." He recalled later that he was embarrassed accepting it, knowing that Robert Culp, his costar, deserved it equally. This was the first of three

Cosby receives his first Emmy award for "I Spy."

Emmies Cosby received for his role in "I Spy," one for each of the show's three seasons before it was dropped by NBC. By that time, though, an important point had been made. A racial barrier had been broken; television would never be the same again.

As Chet Kincaid on "The Bill Cosby Show."

10

A Show of His Own

By the end of 1968, the nation's fascination with spies had passed. "I Spy" was off the air, and it was time for Cosby to do something new. NBC signed him to do a series of specials, and he began to work on the first one.

Three years earlier, when "I Spy" was just beginning, the *New York Times* had written: "When Cosby assumes his role as an undercover agent on television this fall, viewers will get some inkling of how it would be to see Thelonius Monk [the black jazz musician] playing piano in the orchestra of Lawrence Welk. To be sure, Cosby can play a simple melody—as Monk can. But his metier is a sort of free-associative jazz improvisation."[1]

As he began to work on ideas for the first special, Cosby returned to his free-form roots. He decided that there would be no guests on his special; he would do the show solo. The format would have him returning to his old neighborhood in Philadelphia and doing a series of comedy monologues about growing up. It would be a kind of stand-up comedy hour.

After the special was aired, the critics were divided in their reactions, but most felt that Cosby should have had guests on his show. Fifteen years later, television schedules would be filled with comedians doing solo comedy concerts, and Richard Pryor's filmed concerts would be big hits with movie audiences. But in 1968, the format was years ahead of its time.

Richard Pryor

Cosby was stung by the critical reaction to his special, but he didn't dwell on it. There were too many other things to do. He was playing large concert halls around the country and working on a television sitcom for the fall. Also, the minor fluctuations of his career were soon eclipsed by events that were shaking society at large.

Cosby was doing a concert in Kansas City on April 4, 1968, when he learned that Martin Luther King, Jr., had been shot in Memphis. Cosby walked out on stage in a state of shock. He tried to collect himself and do his routines, but after about half an hour, he told the audience that he simply could not go on with the show. For a moment, there was dead silence. Then wave after wave of applause reached the stage. The next day Cosby flew to Memphis to join in a protest march through the city. The day after that, he went to Atlanta for King's funeral.

King's assassination had a profound effect on many Americans, and Bill Cosby was one of them. His "I Spy" role notwithstading, Cosby had never been at the forefront of the civil rights movement, but now he began to think about what he could do to create a better racial climate. In a sense, he'd always tried to do that through his humor; he had stressed the things that the races had in common rather than emphasizing their differences.

Now he thought about all this in connection with his upcoming TV series on NBC. The network executives had wanted him to play a funny detective on the show. Their reasoning was simple: audiences recognized Cosby as a comedian and also as a spy; since funny spies were out of fashion, they went for the closest thing—a funny detective.

Cosby said no to the idea. When he had started out in comedy, people had expected him to tell only racial jokes, and he had refused to do that. Now he had his own ideas about the character he wanted to play. He wanted it to be a schoolteacher, and he told NBC that he wanted the character to be portrayed realistically. In contrast to the one-dimensional characters usually seen on television, the character of Chet Kincaid would be multifaceted. NBC officials were not especially happy with Cosby's ideas, but they knew that they would not be able to change his mind. They knew that Cosby was his own man.

When "The Bill Cosby Show" aired, it was attacked from several sides at once. Some critics attacked the lack of plot in the show, which made it different from the type of sitcom they were used to. Others attacked its lack of racial tension and strife, claiming that Cosby was avoiding tough issues. They wanted to see urban poverty; they didn't want to see the stories of a nice, middle-class bachelor who taught physical education at a relatively calm high school.

Time and again throughout his career, Cosby would face the charge that he was not really representing blacks in a way that reflected their actual experience in society. In truth, most blacks were not living lives like that of Chet Kincaid—or of Cosby's later creation, Dr. Heathcliff Huxtable. But Bill Cosby saw his role differently. In his view, blacks—particularly young blacks—needed role models. Few blacks *were* teachers or doctors, and the middle class *was* more heavily white than black. The point Cosby wanted to make, however, was that such changes were possible. He wanted to show that by breaking with stereotypes, a television show or movie could create a vision of a life to which blacks and whites alike could aspire. He recognized that the road to equality for blacks was a difficult and treacherous one, and sympathized with those forced to travel it. But Cosby himself had demonstrated that it could be done, and he wanted others to try and succeed as well.

Cosby believed firmly that it was up to the viewers, not the critics, to decide the issue. And in the end, the viewers proved him right. By the end of the television season, ''The Bill Cosby Show'' ranked eleventh among all programs. Despite the turbulence enveloping American society in that year of 1969, Cosby had succeeded in presenting a positive role model for blacks. He had also succeeded in providing significant opportunities for talented black actors and film professionals. In the *New York Times,* the black writer A. S. Doc Young commented:

> Bill Cosby, through sheer force of personality and great talent, has created a hit show, perhaps an improbable hit show. . . . Cosby looms tall among hero figures for black kids who need hero figures in the worst way. . . . Meanwhile, he relates in a constructive way to millions of adult viewers of all races. . . . Cosby would not be at his best as a professional civil rights leader, a Black Panther, or the head of a poverty program. But as Bill Cosby—comic, wit, humorist, and storyteller—he is making an important contribution to Afro-Americans, to Americans as a whole. His contribution is not to be taken lightly.[2]

"The Bill Cosby Show" ran until 1971, when Bill Cosby once again had to decide what he was going to do. There was the possibility of another series for NBC, but Cosby was not keen on the idea. For one thing, it would have meant remaining in California. But Cosby felt that Beverly Hills, where he had a home, was not the best place to raise the two children he and Camille now had.

He also wanted to spend more time with his children. His oldest daughter, Erika Ranee, was just entering school, and Cosby believed that it was important that he spend time with her while she was still growing up. He remembered the disappointment he'd felt toward his own father, and he didn't want his children to feel that way about him.

Cosby had another important reason for not wanting to remain in Los Angeles. He had decided to return to college, get his degree, and pursue a doctorate in education. In the past, he had often said that he would leave show business one day and become a teacher. But he kept putting that day off—until now. By returning to college now, he reasoned, he could achieve his personal dream and be able to spend more time with his children. So later that year, he moved the family to a large house he had purchased in Amherst, Massachusetts, and enrolled at the University of Massachusetts there.

Cosby, however, hadn't turned his back on show business completely. Rather, he felt that there must be a way the two could be combined that would make education exciting and entertainment elevating. Throughout the 1970s, he searched for such a way.

As a result, he became involved with "The Electric Company," a children's television program broadcast on

On the set of "The Electric Company."

public television stations around the country. The show was aimed at helping young children develop reading skills. Cosby took a huge cut in pay to work on the show because he believed in its importance.

"The Electric Company" consisted of a series of sketches built around different reading concepts. A group of teachers and reading experts helped write guidelines for the show and told the writers and cast what concepts were most important. But much of the practical work was done by Cosby and the other performers, who made the ideas come to life. Along with "Sesame Street," "The Electric Company" helped pioneer new kinds of programming for children.

Cosby stayed with "The Electric Company" for a few years; then he grew restless. It was time to move on.

11

A Multimedia Sensation

In the 1970s, Bill Cosby's career went through a ka-
leidescope of changes. While still working on television
programs for children and doing nightclub dates, he had
become something else: a "pitchman," or a person who
sells something. Coca Cola, Ford, Kodak, and General
Foods all paid Cosby to go on television and promote
their products. Advertisers felt that people liked Cosby
and would trust what he had to say about the products
he endorsed. They were right. Cosby had broad appeal
with children and adults; he was destined to become one
of the most effective pitchmen ever.

In the meantime, Cosby worked on the "Fat Albert"
cartoon shows, which were based on his comedy routines
about childhood friends. There was also "The New Bill
Cosby Show," and later in the 1970s, "Cos." Both shows
had a variety-style format, with the show broken into
various segments.

Neither show caught on, however, because in the
1970s, the public's taste in humor had shifted once again,
this time back toward a more direct and abrasive style.
Consequently, people were less interested in Cosby's
gentle humor. Comedy walked a thin line between being
funny and being offensive, and television was filled with
situation comedies that made fun of bigotry—both white
and black. "All in the Family," one of the most successful
series of all time, poked fun at Archie Bunker, a white

Performing on "Cos."

bigot, while shows like "Sanford and Son" and "The Jeffersons" poked fun at blacks who were bigots. These situation comedies were considered more "honest" than the old ones because they addressed racial issues in a straightforward manner. Cosby's easygoing style had gone out of fashion.

But Cosby's interests were not limited to television. He had always loved music and now wanted to make and record it. "When I was a kid, around 13 or 14," he once said, "I used to stand outside the Blue Note in Philadelphia en route to playing some ball. This was at matinees, four in the afternoon. I'd see these musicians greet each other, and they were the first people, outside my family, I saw hug. It seemed like everything they said to each other was either hilarious or warm and wonderful; all smiles. It always seemed that these people enjoyed what they were doing."[1]

Cosby's taste had always run toward soul and jazz. When he was growing up, he had listened to local legend C. Sharpe, the famous alto saxophone player, and also to Archie Shepp, Reggie Workman, and Benny Golson. Cosby himself had played the drums as a young man.

From 1968 until the mid-1970s, Cosby released a series of albums. Some were serious jazz albums, on which Cosby sang in a rich baritone. While none were hits, they were all moderately successful.

Then, in 1976, Cosby scored a hit with *Bill Cosby Is Not Himself These Days, Rat Own, Rat Own, Rat Own*. The album featured cuts satirizing popular rhythm-and-blues and funk stars, and several were hits, including, "I Luv Myself Better Than I Luv Myself."

Another area that Cosby chose to explore was film. In 1972, he starred in two films, *Man and Boy* and *Hickey and Boggs*. Although neither film did well at the box office, Cosby remained determined to make a hit movie.

It finally happened in 1974, when Sidney Poitier offered Cosby a starring role in a film he was directing, *Uptown Saturday Night*. The movie was an action-comedy about a factory worker and a cab driver who set out in pursuit of gangsters who have stolen a wallet containing a winning lottery ticket. Cosby agreed to play the cab-driver opposite Poitier's factory worker. Harry Belafonte had a supporting role.

Poitier wanted to make a film that would have a broad appeal to families and one in which blacks played roles other than detectives and crooks. In making *Uptown Saturday Night*, Poitier also gave many blacks in the technical side of the film business a chance to work on a major production.

With Sidney Poitier in A Piece of the Action.

Uptown Saturday Night was a huge hit coast to coast, popular with both black and white audiences. It was funny, with plenty of action scenes and strong black roles, and critics praised Cosby's performance.

Cosby followed up this hit by appearing in two more films directed by Poitier. Again, the films were action-comedies. *Let's Do It Again,* made in 1975, was about two men who become boxing promoters to raise money for a day-care center in their community. *A Piece of the Action,* made in 1977, had the Cosby-Poitier team helping a social worker trying to reach young kids in the ghetto.

Cosby made two more films in the 1970s: *Mother, Jugs and Speed* and *California Suite. Mother, Jugs and Speed* followed the amusing adventures of an ambulance squad, while *California Suite* showed Bill Cosby and Richard Pryor playing two doctors who spend a weekend in an expensive hotel. While neither film was a hit with the critics, both made money at the box office.

Performing in Milwaukee, 1981.

12

Dr. Huxtable

Cosby had spent the 1970s shifting gears. But despite his many successes, no single career path presented itself. By the beginning of the new decade, Bill Cosby was moving fast—but where? Even he wasn't sure.

One thing was clear, however: Cosby was entering middle age. He was in his early forties—still vigorous and healthy—but no longer young. In his book *Time Flies*, he wrote:

> One morning . . . after I had spent the previous day jogging, I woke up and wondered who had come into my bed and put a knife in my right thigh. There was, however, no pain in my left one: it was painlessly paralyzed.
>
> A few days later, when I healed, I went jogging again and the pain returned, this time a knife in my knee. With a burst of machismo, I ignored it and continued to run.
>
> *What's wrong with you?* said one of my legs. *Didn't you hear us when we first spoke to you? The legs go first, so we want to take this opportunity to say goodbye.*[1]

The issue of getting older had become part of Cosby's comedy routine by now. He had always made the stuff of his life the subject of his humor. When he was a father with young children, he had made children and father-hood the centerpiece of his routines. Now that he was reaching middle age, his subject became aging. He joked: "The only good thing about the decline of my memory is that it has brought me closer to my mother, for she and I now forget everything at the same time."[2]

Cosby remained as active as ever, although some of his critics said that he had fallen behind the younger, faster comedians such as Pryor and Eddie Murphy. Pryor

Eddie Murphy

had made a success out of being "crazy"—he would say or do anything, no matter how outrageous. He shocked audiences into laughter, as Lenny Bruce had. And Murphy could be just as outrageous as Pryor. The material of both comedians included routines about sex and drugs, two subjects that Cosby had always avoided. Next to Pryor and Murphy, Cosby began to sound bland.

But many other performers maintained their great respect for Cosby and his gifts. Steve Allen said that Cosby was nothing less than the most gifted monologist of his time. The reason for Cosby's success in touching audiences, Allen said, was that the "Cos" seemed to be able to connect with the child inside everyone.

For his own part, Cosby still had his sights set on greater things. He'd spent the past ten years exploring two areas: education and family entertainment. He'd earned a degree in education and managed to create entertainment on public television and on Saturday mornings that was both educational and fun for children. But he hadn't managed to translate his vision of good, wholesome family entertainment into prime-time television.

Looking at the network schedules, Cosby was disheartened. The shows were filled with violence and stupid humor. The way people were portrayed was unreal. All this made Cosby once again think about doing a show of his own. But what would it be? He decided that he wanted to emphasize the family and the way people really behaved.

At NBC, Cosby's old network, Brandon Tartikoff was the new president. In the past, NBC had generally ranked behind CBS, but ahead of ABC. In the last few years, however, NBC had fallen on hard times, while ABC had grown stronger, leaping ahead of NBC, which was now in last place. Tartikoff desperately wanted to change that.

Tartikoff happened to see Cosby on "The Tonight Show," and as he listened to Cosby do a routine about raising his children, it occurred to Tartikoff that a sitcom focused on these kinds of situations might succeed with viewers. Tartikoff approached Cosby, and they discussed the type of show that Cosby wanted to do. Both men agreed that it would be a situation comedy that focused on the difficulties of raising a family.

Some people in the business doubted that Cosby could make the show work, particularly after hearing the concept. For the most part, blacks had been portrayed on television as poor and disadvantaged. This had been changing, but slowly. In the mid-1970s, Redd Foxx played a black junkyard owner in "Sanford and Son." In the show, Fred Sanford and his son had lived in Watts, a poor black area of Los Angeles. Later in the decade, "The Jeffersons," a successful spin-off from "All in the Family," portrayed a black family that had made it into the upper-middle class—but most of the humor came out of their discomfort with their new status. In fact, a main source of the humor in "The Jeffersons" was the notion that blacks and prosperity are a strange combination.

Now Cosby was proposing a show that would be completely different. Cosby intended to play a black doctor whose income and lifestyle were decidedly upper-middle class. Network executives feared that no one would want to watch a situation comedy about an upper-middle class black family that was comfortable with its status. Both blacks and whites might resent the good fortune of the characters on the show. Viewers might think the show did not represent the way things really were.

Actually, Cosby had originally intended to play a less well-to-do character on the show. It was his wife, Camille, however, who encouraged him to create the character of Dr. Heathcliff Huxtable for the show. Her encouragement, and Cosby's own feeling that television audiences were ready to accept a less stereotypical black character, encouraged Cosby to take a new tack. He would show things not perhaps as they were but, instead, the way they ought to be.

This would be a new frontier, both for Cosby professionally and for the portrayal of minorities on American television. It was a chance for Cosby to make a sitcom about a black family in exactly the same way that comedies were made about whites—where the situation, and not the racial jokes, supplied the humor. It was an experiment in a new kind of equality, and Cosby felt that America was ready for it.

As the start of the television season approached, - tensions were again running high at NBC. Would the show succeed or would it bomb? Newspapers and magazines were asking the same question. Many of them predicted that Americans would not accept "The Cosby Show," that it would fall flat on its face because it was just too big a step from "The Jeffersons" and other black sitcoms.

Cosby, the cast, and the writers, however, were too busy creating the show to bother with the doubters. They were working hard to polish the scripts and make each show work so that when "The Cosby Show" finally aired on September 20, 1984, all questions would be laid to rest.

The show was a smash success. Americans of all colors and backgrounds recognized themselves in the Huxtable family. The gentle humor about family life was appealing precisely because it wasn't based on racial jokes or stereotypes, but on sound writing about common daily problems.

"The Cosby Show" quickly went to the number one spot in the ratings and pushed NBC to the same position among the networks. Some critics said that Americans would soon tire of the show. But as the season wore on, viewers continued to watch in record numbers. The show's stories and characters simply rang true. The situations seemed honest and funny at the same time.

At the end of the first season, "The Cosby Show" swept all its categories in the Emmy Awards. And in the seasons that followed, it consistently remained one of the ten most popular shows on television. Bill Cosby had

With Earle Hyman and Malcolm-Jamal Warner on "The Cosby Show."

proven to the world that people could respond to blacks as real people in real situations. And more importantly, he had educated a nation—he had made people understand that color barriers can be dissolved.

Making his point through humor, Cosby helped create a new image for blacks, which was a very important achievement. Sociologists and educators alike often speak of role models, people whom others can look up to and emulate. But role models can be positive or negative. In the Huxtables, Cosby and his creative team developed a lifestyle and a set of family relationships that were calculated to be positive. Audiences liked Cliff Huxtable not because he was black, and not because he was funny (although he was), but because he seemed real and admirable.

13

The Benefactor

With "The Cosby Show" a smash hit, viewers might have expected Bill Cosby to rest on his laurels. But he didn't. While working very hard on each segment of "The Cosby Show," he still found time for new ventures. First, in 1987, there was a movie. Because of his show's huge popularity, Cosby had been hounded by major producers who wanted to feature him in a film. Cosby was given almost total financial and artistic control, as well as the starring role, in *Leonard, Part 6*, a big-budget secret-agent spoof. The movie bombed.

Somewhat humbled by that experience, Cosby focused his attention on writing instead. He wrote three books in the 1980s—*Fatherhood, Time Flies,* and *Love and Marriage*—all of which made the best-seller list. He also continued to do club dates in Las Vegas. And in 1990, he made another film, *Ghost Dad*, directed by his friend, Sidney Poitier.

These activities paled next to Cosby's interest in education, however. In many ways, his gift to Spelman College was the high point of his career.

Bill Cosby had always given a great deal of himself during the more than twenty-five years he had spent as an entertainer. He'd triumphed as a comedian, broken down barriers for blacks in network television, and by using humor had built bridges of understanding between people of all races. In making his donation of $20

Dick Gregory applauds Cosby's honorary degree from Morehouse.

million to the black women's college, however, he had made it clear that his commitment to society was deep and heartfelt.

The donation was the largest ever given by an individual to a black college, and was the fourth largest individual donation to any college in history. The money would be used to build an academic center, a women's center, an audiovisual center, and faculty offices; in addition, some of it would be used to endow chairs in the fine arts, social sciences, and humanities. The donation would transform the campus of the 107-year-old school.

In Cosby's speech to the crowd, he said that he wanted the donation to signal to the nation that "some serious stuff [is] going on down here."[1] He reminded his listeners that slaves had once met and learned to read in the basements of some of the buildings on the campus. His point was that the same urge to better one's life in the face of impossible odds exists in all people. It lay in the foundation of Spelman College. And it underlay Bill Cosby's entire career.

Over the next few months, newspapers and magazines all over the nation carried the news of Cosby's gift to Spelman. Headlines referred to the Cosbys as the "First Family of Philanthropy" and called the gift "A Source of Funds and Hope."

The youngster growing up in the streets of Germantown could never have imagined himself a wealthy benefactor or an educator of millions. But the earnest, loving example of his mother, along with the troubling experience of growing up black in a white world, had combined to form an unusual person, a person who made people laugh but who also took laughter very seriously.

Important Events in Bill Cosby's Life

1937	Born on July 12 in Philadelphia, Pennsylvania.
1952	Drops out of Germantown High School.
1956	Joins the navy.
1960	Enters Temple University.
1961	Begins to develop a comedy act.
1962	Works at the Gaslight in New York; drops out of Temple.
1963	Appears on "The Tonight Show."
1964	Marries Camille Hanks.
1965	Gets costarring role in "I Spy."
1966	Receives Emmy Award for "I Spy."
1969	"The Bill Cosby Show" airs.
1974	Stars in *Uptown Saturday Night.*
1984	"The Cosby Show" first airs on September 20.
1985	His first book, *Fatherhood,* is published.
1987	*Time Flies* is published.
1988	Donates $20 million to Spelman College.
1989	*Love and Marriage* is published.
1990	Stars in *Ghost Dad,* directed by Sidney Poitier.

Notes

Chapter 1

1 "The President's Report, 1988," *Spelman Messenger*, pp. 12-13.

2 "The President's Report," pp. 12-13.

3 Monica Collins, "Talking with Cos," *Ladies Home Journal*, January 1988.

4 Collins.

Chapter 2

1 Ronald L. Smith, *Cosby* (New York: St. Martin's Press, 1986), p. 4.

2 James Haskins, *Bill Cosby: America's Most Famous Father* (New York: Walker and Co., 1988), p. 2.

Chapter 3

1 Haskins, p. 20.

2 Haskins, p. 17.

3 Haskins, p. 16.

Chapter 5

1 Haskins, p. 32.

Chapter 6

1 Joseph Dorinson and Joseph Boskin, "Racial and Ethnic Humor," in *Humor in America*, ed. by Joseph E. Mintz (Westport, Conn.: Greenwood Press, 1988), p. 178.

2 Dorinson and Boskin, p. 178.

Chapter 7

1 Haskins, p. 35.

2 Smith, p. 35.

Chapter 8

1 Smith, p. 52.

Chapter 10

1 Charles L. Mee, Jr., "That's the Truth—and Other Cosby Stories," *New York Times*, March 14, 1965.

2 A.S. Doc Young, "Bill Cosby Is Not Malcolm X, He's Bill Cosby," *New York Times*, December 21, 1969.

Chapter 11

1 Michael Bourne, "Bill Cosby Loves Jazz!," *Down Beat*, July 1988.

Chapter 12

1 Bill Cosby, *Time Flies* (New York: Doubleday, 1987), pp. 37-38.

2 Cosby, *Time Flies*, p. 83.

Chapter 13

1 "The President's Report," p. 13.

Suggested Reading

Cosby, Bill. *Fatherhood*. New York: Doubleday, 1985.

Cosby, Bill. *Time Flies*. New York: Doubleday, 1987.

Cosby, Bill. *Love and Marriage*. New York: Doubleday, 1989.

Haskins, James, *Richard Pryor: A Man and His Madness*. New York, Beaufort Books, 1984.

Quayle, Louise, *Martin Luther King, Jr.: Dreams for a Nation*. New York: Ballantine Books, 1989.

Smith, Ronald L. *Cosby*. New York: St. Martin's Press, 1986.

Twain, Mark. *The Complete Short Stories of Mark Twain*. New York: Bantam, 1957.

Zadra, Dan. *The Cosby Show*. Mankato, Minn.: Creative Education, 1986.

Index